Brownies Cookbook: Delicious Brownie Recipes

Homemade Brownies

Book 1

Delectable & Easy Brownies for Kids, Friends, and Family

Legal & Disclaimer

The information contained in this book and its contents is not designed to replace or take the place of any form of medical or professional advice; and is not meant to replace the need for independent medical, financial, legal or other professional advice or services, as may be required. The content and information in this book has been provided for educational and entertainment purposes only.

The content and information contained in this book has been compiled from sources deemed reliable, and it is accurate to the best of the Author's knowledge, information, and belief. However, the Author cannot guarantee its accuracy and validity and cannot be held liable for any errors and/or omissions. Further, changes are periodically made to this book as and when needed. Where appropriate and/or necessary, you must consult a professional (including but not limited to your doctor, attorney, financial advisor or such other professional advisor) before using any of the suggested remedies, techniques, or information in this book.

Upon using the contents and information contained in this book, you agree to hold harmless the Author from and against any damages, costs, and expenses, including any legal fees potentially resulting from the application of any of the information provided by this book. This disclaimer applies to any loss, damages or injury caused by the use and application, whether directly or indirectly, of any advice or information presented, whether for breach of contract, tort, negligence, personal injury, criminal intent, or under any other cause of action.

You agree to accept all risks of using the information presented in this book.

You agree that by continuing to read this book, where appropriate and/or necessary, you shall consult a professional (including but not limited to your doctor, attorney, or financial advisor or such other advisor as needed) before using any of the suggested remedies, techniques, or information in this book.

ISBN: 9781093800692

About This Cookbook

This cookbook contains mouth-watering brownies that will help you to prepare delicious brownies for your kids, friends, and family. In this cookbook you will find traditional brownie recipes as well as brownie–muffins recipes.

Enjoy various tastes and colors brownies. Every reader will find something mouth-watering for himself. This book contains a collection of **40 brownie recipes**.

You don't need to be a professional 28 Michelin Star chef to cook tasty brownie desserts from this cookbook and to prepare colorful brownies for yourself or your family. I would like to suggest to test these brownie recipes and to experiment with the ingredients adding your own tastes and flavors!

Kitchen Tools That You Will Need to Prepare Brownies

To prepare delicious brownies you will need to have the right utensils in your kitchen. The following list of kitchen tools will help you.

Food scale

The food scale is the main tool. You will use it to measure any food and it will always show you the quantity of ingredients that you need for brownies.

Food processor or blender

Having a food processor or blender is important. It will help you to process, pulse, and blend brownie ingredients.

Electric hand mixer

Electric hand mixer will save your energy and of course time, especially when preparing brownie recipes where you often need to combine various ingredients.

Silicone molds or muffin cups

Silicone molds, muffin cups, baking cups are crucial when preparing brownies because you will need them to bake or to store brownies.

Pot or saucepan

Having a large pot, saucepan or bowl in your kitchen is crucial for preparing brownies because you will melt, mix, combine, keep and boil all the ingredients there.

Knife sharpening stone or sharp knife

When preparing brownies you often need to cut, slice or halve some ingredients. In this case, having a sharp blade in your kitchen will save you a lot of time and frustrations because you will finish cutting up your fruits and other ingredients much faster than you would if using a dull knife.

Parchment paper

Parchment paper or baking paper will be very helpful in your brownies journey because it will help you to bake delicious brownies.

Baking pan

Baking pan is important because you will bake your brownies there.

Potato masher

Yes! You are right; we will need a potato masher to prepare tasty brownies. No, we won't mash the potatoes, but fruits and berries!

The following chapters contain delicious brownie recipes that will have your taste buds come to life!

1. Pineapple Peanut Brownies

Prep Time: 10 min | Cooking & Baking Time: 1 hour 10 min | Servings: 4

Ingredients:

- 1 cup of peanuts, ground
- 1 cup pineapple, peeled and cubed
- 2 tablespoons pure pineapple extract
- 5 tablespoons cocoa powder
- 1 cup of unsweetened cooking chocolate (70-95%)
- 2 eggs
- 3 tablespoons coconut butter
- 5 tablespoons sugar

- 1 teaspoon baking powder

- spray cream

- baking spray

Instructions:

1. Preheat the oven to 300°-320°Fahrenheit and roast the peanuts in the oven for 10 minutes until lightly browned and crispy and set aside to cool completely. Then grind the peanuts using a food processor.

2. Spoon the coconut butter and sugar into a food processor and blend until homogenous mass. Then stir in the peanuts and mix well.

3. Melt the cooking chocolate in a double boiler for 10 minutes.

4. Mix in the pure pineapple extract, cocoa powder, eggs, and baking powder and blend all the ingredients and mixtures using a food processor until they have a smooth and creamy consistency. Add in the pineapple cubes and mix until homogenous mass.

5. Preheat the oven to 280°-300° Fahrenheit and then coat the baking pan with the baking spray.

6. Spoon the sweet pineapple peanut brownies mixture into the baking pan and bake for 50 minutes at 300°-320°Fahrenheit.

7. Then cool the pineapple peanut brownies, cut them into squares and serve with the spray cream on top. Remember that these tasty pineapple peanut brownies should be served cold with tea or coffee.

Nutrients per serving:

Net Carbs: 9g; Total Fat: 28g; Protein: 15g; Calories: 231

2. Pineapple Walnut Brownies

Prep Time: 10 min | Cooking & Baking Time: 1 hour 10 min | Servings: 4

Ingredients:

- 1 cup of walnuts, ground

- 1 cup of pineapple, peeled and cubed

- 2 tablespoons pure pineapple extract

- 5 tablespoons cocoa powder

- 1 cup of unsweetened cooking chocolate (70-95%)

- 2 eggs

- 3 tablespoons coconut butter

- 5 tablespoons sugar

- 1 teaspoon baking powder

- spray cream

- baking spray

Instructions:

1. Preheat the oven to 300°-320°Fahrenheit and roast the walnuts in the oven for 10 minutes until lightly browned and crispy and set aside to cool completely. Then grind the walnuts using a food processor.

2. Spoon the coconut butter and sugar into a food processor and blend until homogenous mass. Then stir in the walnuts and mix well.

3. Mix in the pure pineapple extract, cocoa powder, eggs, and baking powder and blend all the ingredients using a food processor until they have a smooth and creamy consistency. Add in the pineapple cubes and mix until homogenous mass. Melt the cooking chocolate in a double boiler for 10 minutes and combine with all the ingredients.

4. Preheat the oven to 280°-300° Fahrenheit and then coat the silicone molds or muffin cups with the baking spray.

5. Spoon the sweet pineapple walnut brownies mixture into the silicone molds or muffin cups and bake for 50 minutes at 300°- 320°Fahrenheit.

6. Then cool the pineapple walnut brownies and serve with the spray cream on top. Remember that these tasty pineapple walnuts brownies should be served cool.

Nutrients per serving:

Net Carbs: 10g; Total Fat: 29g; Protein: 15g; Calories: 261

3. Peanut Mango Brownies

Prep Time: 10 min | Cooking & Baking Time: 50 min | Servings: 4

Ingredients:

- 1 cup of peanuts, ground
- 1 mango, cubed
- 3 tablespoons pure mango extract
- 5 tablespoons cocoa powder
- 4 tablespoons unsalted butter
- 1 cup of unsweetened cooking chocolate (70-95%)
- 5 tablespoons coconut oil
- 2 teaspoons baking powder

- 5 tablespoons sugar

- 1 teaspoon cinnamon

- baking spray

Instructions:

1. Preheat the oven to 300°-320°Fahrenheit and roast the peanuts in the oven for 10 minutes until lightly browned and crispy and then set aside to cool completely. Then grind the peanuts using a food processor.

2. Melt the cooking chocolate in a double boiler for 10 minutes and then stir in the other ingredients and mix well using a hand mixer.

3. Preheat the oven to 280°-300° Fahrenheit and then coat the muffin cups or candy cups with the baking spray.

4. Pour the mixture into the muffin cups or candy cups and bake for around 40 minutes and then you are free to serve. Remember that these delicious peanut mango brownies should be served warm.

Nutrients per serving:

Net Carbs: 12g; Total Fat: 20g; Protein: 9g; Calories: 187

4. Peanut Banana Brownies

Prep Time: 10 min | Cooking & Baking Time: 50 min | Servings: 4

Ingredients:

- 1 cup of peanuts, ground
- 1 banana, cubed
- 3 tablespoons pure banana extract
- 5 tablespoons cocoa powder
- 4 tablespoons unsalted butter
- 1 cup of unsweetened cooking chocolate (70-95%)
- 2 eggs
- 1 cup of flour
- 5 tablespoons coconut oil
- 2 teaspoons baking powder
- 5 tablespoons sugar
- 1 teaspoon vanilla
- baking spray

Instructions:

1. Preheat the oven to 300°-320°Fahrenheit and roast the peanuts in the oven for 10 minutes until lightly browned and

crispy and then set aside to cool completely. Then grind the peanuts using a food processor or blender.

2. Beat the eggs with the sugar using a hand mixer until the mixture becomes foamy and grows in volume at least two times.

3. Add the flour and beat the eggs mixture for 10 minutes more. Then mix in the baking powder.

4. Melt the cooking chocolate in a double boiler for 10 minutes and then stir in the other ingredients and mix well using a hand mixer.

5. Preheat the oven to 280°-300° Fahrenheit and then coat the baking pan with the baking spray.

6. Pour the mixture into the baking pan and bake for around 40 minutes, cut the mixture into squares and then you are free to serve. Remember that these delicious peanut banana brownies should be served warm.

Nutrients per serving:

Net Carbs: 12g; Total Fat: 22g; Protein: 9g; Calories: 188

5. Peanut Raspberry Brownies

Prep Time: 10 min | Cooking & Baking Time: 50 min | Servings: 4

Ingredients:

- 1 cup of peanuts, ground
- 1 cup of fresh raspberries
- 3 tablespoons pure raspberry extract
- 5 tablespoons cocoa powder
- 4 tablespoons unsalted butter
- 1 cup of unsweetened cooking chocolate (70-95%)
- 5 tablespoons coconut oil
- 2 teaspoons baking powder

- 5 tablespoons sugar

- 1 teaspoon vanilla

- baking spray

Instructions:

1. Preheat the oven to 300°-320°Fahrenheit and roast the peanuts in the oven for 10 minutes until lightly browned and crispy and then set aside to cool completely. Then grind the peanuts using a food processor.

2. Combine the raspberries with the sugar and mash the berries using the potato masher. Then melt the cooking chocolate in a double boiler for 10 minutes and stir in the other ingredients and mix well using a hand mixer.

3. Preheat the oven to 280°-300° Fahrenheit and then coat the baking pan with the baking spray.

4. Pour the mixture into the baking pan and bake for around 40 minutes and then you are free to serve. Remember that these delicious peanut raspberry brownies should be served warm.

Nutrients per serving:

Net Carbs: 12g; Total Fat: 22g; Protein: 9g; Calories: 188

6. Peanut Strawberry Brownies

Prep Time: 10 min | Cooking & Baking Time: 50 min | Servings: 4

Ingredients:

- 1 cup of peanuts, ground
- 1 cup of fresh strawberries
- 3 tablespoons pure strawberry extract
- 5 tablespoons cocoa powder
- 4 tablespoons unsalted butter
- 1 cup of unsweetened cooking chocolate (70-95%)
- 5 tablespoons coconut oil
- 2 teaspoons baking powder
- 5 tablespoons sugar
- 1 teaspoon vanilla
- baking spray

Instructions:

1. Preheat the oven to 300°-320°Fahrenheit and roast the peanuts in the oven for 10 minutes until lightly browned and crispy then set aside to cool completely. Then grind the peanuts using a food processor.

2. Combine the strawberries with the sugar and mash the berries using a potato masher. Then melt the cooking

chocolate in a double boiler for 10 minutes and stir in the other ingredients and mix well using a hand mixer.

3. Preheat the oven to 280°-300° Fahrenheit and then coat the muffin cups or candy cups with the baking spray.

5. Pour the mixture into the muffin cups or candy cups and bake for around 40 minutes and then you are free to serve. Remember that these tasty and sweet peanut strawberry brownies should be served warm.

Nutrients per serving:

Net Carbs: 12g; Total Fat: 22g; Protein: 9g; Calories: 188

7. Peanut Blueberry Brownies

Prep Time: 10 min | Cooking & Baking Time: 50 min | Servings: 4

Ingredients:

- 1 cup of peanuts, ground
- 1 cup of fresh blueberries
- 2 tablespoons pure blueberry extract
- 5 tablespoons cocoa powder
- 4 tablespoons unsalted butter
- 1 cup of unsweetened cooking chocolate (70-95%)
- 5 tablespoons coconut oil
- 2 teaspoons baking powder

- 5 tablespoons sugar

- 1 teaspoon vanilla

- baking spray

Instructions:

1. Preheat the oven to 300°-320°Fahrenheit and roast the peanuts in the oven for 10 minutes until lightly browned and crispy and then set aside to cool completely. Then grind the peanuts using a food processor or blender.

2. Combine the blueberries with the sugar and mash the berries using the potato masher. Then melt the cooking chocolate in a double boiler for 10 minutes and stir in the other ingredients and mix well using a hand mixer.

3. Preheat the oven to 280°-300° Fahrenheit and then coat the baking pan with the baking spray.

4. Pour the mixture into the baking pan and bake for around 40 minutes and then cut the mixture into squares and you are free to serve. Pour some chocolate syrup on top. Remember that these tasty peanut blueberry brownies should be served warm.

Nutrients per serving:

Net Carbs: 13g; Total Fat: 24g; Protein: 9g; Calories: 193

8.   Vanilla Strawberry Brownies

Prep Time: 20 min | Cooking & Baking Time: 50 min | Servings: 4

Ingredients:

- 1 cup of strawberry jam
- 3 tablespoons pure strawberry extract
- 5 tablespoons cocoa powder
- 4 tablespoons unsalted butter
- 2 eggs
- 1 cup of flour
- 1 cup of unsweetened cooking chocolate (70-95%)
- 5 tablespoons coconut oil
- 2 teaspoons baking powder
- 5 tablespoons sugar
- 2 teaspoons pure vanilla extract
- baking spray

Instructions:

1. Combine the strawberry jam with the half of the sugar and pure strawberry extract and mix well.

2. Beat the eggs with the sugar using a hand mixer until the mixture becomes foamy and grows in volume at least two times.

3. Add the flour and beat the eggs mixture for 10 minutes more. Then mix in the baking powder.

4. Then melt the cooking chocolate in a double boiler for 10 minutes and add in the other ingredients and mix well using a hand mixer or blender.

5. Preheat the oven to 300°-320° Fahrenheit and then coat the muffin cups or candy cups with the baking spray.

6. Pour the mixture into the muffin cups or candy cups and bake for around 40 minutes and then you are free to serve. Remember that these sweet vanilla strawberry brownies should be served warm with the cappuccino.

Nutrients per serving:

Net Carbs: 13g; Total Fat: 19g; Protein: 8g; Calories: 178

9. Banana Walnut Brownies

Prep Time: 20 min | Cooking & Baking Time: 1 hour 10 min | Servings: 4

Ingredients:

- 1 cup of walnuts, ground
- 2 bananas, peeled and cubed
- 2 tablespoons pure banana extract
- 5 tablespoons cocoa powder
- 1 cup of unsweetened cooking chocolate (70-95%)
- 2 eggs
- 1 cup of white flour
- 3 tablespoons coconut butter

- 5 tablespoons sugar

- 1 teaspoon baking powder

- spray cream

- baking spray

Instructions:

1. Preheat the oven to 300°-320°Fahrenheit and roast the walnuts in the oven for 10 minutes until lightly browned and crispy and then set aside to cool completely. Then grind the walnuts using a food processor or blender.

2. Spoon the coconut butter and half of the sugar into a food processor and blend until homogenous mass. Then stir in the walnuts and mix well.

3. Beat the eggs with the sugar using a hand mixer until the mixture becomes foamy and grows in volume at least two times.

4. Add the flour and beat the eggs mixture for 10 minutes more. Then mix in the baking powder.

5. Melt the cooking chocolate in a double boiler for 10 minutes.

6. Mix in the pure banana extract, cocoa powder and blend all the ingredients using a food processor until they have a smooth and creamy consistency. Add in the banana cubes and mix until homogenous mass.

7. Preheat the oven to 300°-320° Fahrenheit and then coat the silicone molds or muffin cups with the baking spray.

8. Spoon the sweet banana walnut brownies mixture into the silicone molds or muffin cups and bake for 50 minutes at 300°- 320°Fahrenheit.

9. Then cool the banana walnut brownies and serve with the spray cream on top. Remember that these banana walnut brownies should be served cold with the cup of tea or cocoa.

Nutrients per serving:

Net Carbs: 10g; Total Fat: 29g; Protein: 14g; Calories: 229

10. Coconut Brownies

Prep Time: 20 min | Cooking & Baking Time: 1 hour 10 min | Servings: 4

Ingredients:

- 1 cup of shredded coconut
- 2 tablespoons pure coconut extract
- 5 tablespoons cocoa powder
- 1 cup of unsweetened cooking chocolate (70-95%)
- 2 eggs
- 1 cup of flour
- 5 tablespoons coconut butter
- 5 tablespoons sugar
- 1 teaspoon baking powder
- spray cream
- baking spray

Instructions:

1. Preheat the oven to 300°-320°Fahrenheit and roast the shredded coconut in the oven for 10 minutes until lightly browned.

2. Spoon the coconut butter and half of the sugar into a food processor and blend until homogenous mass. Then stir in the shredded coconut and mix well.

3. Beat the eggs with the sugar using a hand mixer until the mixture becomes foamy and grows in volume at least two times.

4. Add the flour and beat the eggs mixture for 10 minutes more. Then mix in the baking powder.

5. Melt the cooking chocolate in a double boiler for 10 minutes.

6. Mix in the pure coconut extract, cocoa powder, eggs, and baking powder and blend all the ingredients using a food processor until they have a smooth and creamy consistency.

7. Preheat the oven to 300°-320° Fahrenheit and then coat the silicone molds or muffin cups with the baking spray.

8. Spoon the coconut brownies mixture into the silicone molds or muffin cups and bake for 50 minutes at 300°-320°Fahrenheit.

9. Then cool the coconut brownies and serve with the spray cream on top. Remember that these coconut brownies should be served cold with the cup of tea or hot chocolate.

Nutrients per serving:

Net Carbs: 10g; Total Fat: 28g; Protein: 15g; Calories: 231

11. Raspberry Brownies

Prep Time: 15 min | Cooking & Baking Time: 1 hour 10 min | Servings: 4

Ingredients:

- 1 cup of raspberry jelly

- 2 tablespoons pure raspberry extract

- 5 tablespoons cocoa powder

- 1 cup of unsweetened cooking chocolate (70-95%)

- 2 eggs

- 5 tablespoons unsalted butter

- 5 tablespoons sugar

- 1 teaspoon baking powder

- baking spray

Instructions:

1. Combine the unsalted butter and sugar in a food processor and blend until homogenous mass.

2. Melt the cooking chocolate in a double boiler for 10 minutes and then stir in the baking powder and mix well using a hand mixer.

3. Mix in the pure raspberry extract, raspberry jelly, cocoa powder, and eggs and blend all the ingredients using a food processor until they have a smooth and creamy consistency.

4. Preheat the oven to 300°-320° Fahrenheit and then coat the baking pan with the baking spray.

5. Spoon the raspberry brownies mixture into the baking pan and bake for 50 minutes at 300°- 320°Fahrenheit.

6. Then cool the raspberry brownies, cut into squares and serve. Remember that these raspberry brownies should be served cold with the cup of tea or hot chocolate.

Nutrients per serving:

Net Carbs: 11g; Total Fat: 33g; Protein: 18g; Calories: 239

12.   Strawberry Brownies

Prep Time: 20 min | Cooking & Baking Time: 1 hour 10 min | Servings: 4

Ingredients:

- 1 cup of strawberry jam
- 2 tablespoons pure strawberry extract
- 5 tablespoons cocoa powder
- 1 cup of unsweetened cooking chocolate (70-95%)
- 2 eggs
- 1 cup of flour
- 5 tablespoons unsalted butter
- 5 tablespoons sugar
- 1 teaspoon baking powder
- baking spray

Instructions:

1. Combine the unsalted butter and half of the sugar in a food processor and blend until homogenous mass.

2. Beat the eggs with the sugar using a hand mixer until the mixture becomes foamy and grows in volume at least two times.

3. Add the flour and beat the eggs mixture for 10 minutes more. Then mix in the baking powder.

4. Mix in the pure strawberry extract, strawberry jam, cocoa powder, and blend all the ingredients using a food processor until they have a smooth and creamy consistency.

5. Melt the cooking chocolate in a double boiler for 10 minutes and then stir in the other ingredients and mix well using a hand mixer or food processor.

6. Preheat the oven to 300°-320° Fahrenheit and then coat the silicone molds or muffin cups with the baking spray.

7. Spoon the strawberry brownies mixture into the silicone molds or muffin cups and bake for 50 minutes at 300°-320° Fahrenheit.

8. Then cool the strawberry brownies and serve. Remember that these strawberry brownies should be served cold with the cup of tea or hot chocolate.

Nutrients per serving:

Net Carbs: 13g; Total Fat: 27g; Protein: 18g; Calories: 228

13. Fresh Strawberry Brownies

Prep Time: 15 min | Cooking & Baking Time: 50 min | Servings: 4

Ingredients:

- 1 cup of fresh strawberries

- 2 tablespoons pure strawberry extract

- 5 tablespoons cocoa powder

- 4 tablespoons unsalted butter

- 1 cup of unsweetened cooking chocolate (70-95%)

- 1 cup of flour

- 3 eggs

- 2 teaspoons baking powder

- 5 tablespoons sugar

- 1 teaspoon vanilla

- baking spray

Instructions:

1. Combine the strawberries with the half of sugar and mash the berries using a potato masher and then set aside for 30 minutes.

2. Beat the eggs with the sugar using a hand mixer until the mixture becomes foamy and grows in volume at least two times.

3. Add the flour and beat the eggs mixture for 10 minutes more. Then mix in the baking powder.

4. Melt the cooking chocolate in a double boiler for 10 minutes and stir in the other ingredients and mix well using a hand mixer.

5. Preheat the oven to 280°-300° Fahrenheit and then coat the muffin cups or candy cups with the baking spray.

6. Pour the mixture into the muffin cups or candy cups and bake for around 40 minutes and then you are free to serve. Remember that these tasty and sweet fresh strawberry brownies should be served warm.

Nutrients per serving:

Net Carbs: 13g; Total Fat: 23g; Protein: 10g; Calories: 179

14.   Blueberry Brownies

Prep Time: 10 min | Cooking & Baking Time: 50 min | Servings: 4

Ingredients:

- 1 cup of fresh blueberries
- 1 cup of blueberry jam
- 1 tablespoon pure blueberry extract
- 5 tablespoons cocoa powder
- 4 tablespoons unsalted butter
- 1 cup of unsweetened cooking chocolate (70-95%)
- 5 tablespoons coconut oil
- 2 teaspoons baking powder
- 3 tablespoons sugar
- 1 teaspoon vanilla
- baking spray

Instructions:

1. Combine the blueberries with the sugar and mash the berries using a potato masher and then set aside for 30 minutes.

2. Melt the cooking chocolate in a double boiler for 10 minutes and stir in the other ingredients and mix well using a hand mixer.

3. Preheat the oven to 280°-300° Fahrenheit and then coat the baking pan with the baking spray.

4. Pour the mixture into the baking pan and bake for around 40 minutes and then you are free to serve. Remember that these tasty and sweet fresh blueberry brownies should be served warm.

Nutrients per serving:

Net Carbs: 12.5g; Total Fat: 23g; Protein: 10.5g; Calories: 181

15. Blueberry Orange Brownies

Prep Time: 10 min | Cooking & Baking Time: 50 min | Servings: 4

Ingredients:

- 1 cup of blueberry jam

- 2 tablespoons orange zest, minced

- 1 tablespoon pure orange extract

- 5 tablespoons cocoa powder

- 5 tablespoons unsalted butter

- 1 cup of unsweetened cooking chocolate (70-95%)

- 2 teaspoons baking powder

- 3 tablespoons sugar

- 1 teaspoon vanilla

- baking spray

Instructions:

1. Combine the blueberry jam with the sugar and orange zest and mash the berries using a potato masher and then set aside for 30 minutes.

2. Melt the cooking chocolate in a double boiler for 10 minutes and add in the other ingredients and mix well using a hand mixer.

3. Preheat the oven to 280°-300° Fahrenheit and then coat the parchment paper with the baking spray.

4. Spoon the mixture on the parchment paper and bake for around 40 minutes and then cut the mixture into squares and you are free to serve. Remember that these mouth-watering and sweet blueberry orange brownies should be served warm.

Nutrients per serving:

Net Carbs: 12.7g; Total Fat: 24g; Protein: 10.7g; Calories: 179

16. Raspberry Orange Brownies

Prep Time: 10 min | Cooking & Baking Time: 50 min | Servings: 4

Ingredients:

- 1 cup of raspberry jelly
- 2 tablespoons orange zest, minced
- 1 tablespoon pure orange extract
- 5 tablespoons cocoa powder
- 5 tablespoons unsalted butter
- 3 eggs
- 1 cup of flour
- 1 cup of unsweetened cooking chocolate (70-95%)
- 2 teaspoons baking powder
- 3 tablespoons sugar
- 1 teaspoon vanilla
- baking spray

Instructions:

1. Combine the raspberries with the half of sugar and orange zest and mash the berries using a potato masher and then set aside for 30 minutes.

2. Beat the eggs with the sugar using a hand mixer until the mixture becomes foamy and grows in volume at least two times.

3. Add the flour and beat the eggs mixture for 10 minutes more. Then mix in the baking powder.

4. Melt the cooking chocolate in a double boiler for 10 minutes and add in the other ingredients and mix well using a hand mixer.

5. Preheat the oven to 280°-300° Fahrenheit and then coat the parchment paper with the baking spray.

6. Spoon the mixture on the parchment paper and bake for around 40 minutes and then you are free to serve. Remember that these mouth-watering and sweet raspberry orange brownies should be served warm.

Nutrients per serving:

Net Carbs: 12.7g; Total Fat: 24g; Protein: 10.7g; Calories: 179

17. Strawberry Orange Brownies

Prep Time: 10 min | Cooking & Baking Time: 50 min | Servings: 4

Ingredients:

- 1 cup of strawberry

- 2 tablespoons orange zest, minced

- 1 tablespoon pure orange extract

- 5 tablespoons cocoa powder

- 5 tablespoons unsalted butter

- 3 eggs

- 1 cup of flour

- 1 cup of unsweetened cooking chocolate (70-95%)

- 2 teaspoons baking powder

- 3 tablespoons sugar

- 1 teaspoon vanilla

- baking spray

Instructions:

1. Combine the strawberries with the half of sugar and orange zest and mash the berries using a potato masher and then set aside for 30 minutes.

2. Beat the eggs with the sugar using a hand mixer until the mixture becomes foamy and grows in volume at least two times.

3. Add the flour and beat the eggs mixture for 10 minutes more. Then mix in the baking powder.

4. Melt the cooking chocolate in a double boiler for 10 minutes and add in the other ingredients and mix well using a hand mixer.

5. Preheat the oven to 280°-300° Fahrenheit and then coat the parchment paper with the baking spray.

6. Spoon the mixture on the parchment paper and bake for around 40 minutes and then cut it into squares and you are free to serve. Remember that these delicious and sweet strawberry orange brownies should be served warm.

Nutrients per serving:

Net Carbs: 12.5g; Total Fat: 23g; Protein: 9.7g; Calories: 185

18. Walnut Vanilla Brownies

Prep Time: 10 min | Cooking & Baking Time: 1 hour | Servings: 4

Ingredients:

- 1 cup of walnuts

- 2 tablespoons pure vanilla extract

- 5 tablespoons unsalted butter

- 1 cup of unsweetened cooking chocolate (70-95%)

- 2 eggs

- 1 cup of flour

- 5 tablespoons coconut oil

- 2 teaspoons baking powder

- 1 cup of sugar

- baking spray

Instructions:

1. Preheat the oven to 300°-320°Fahrenheit and roast the walnuts in the oven for 10 minutes until lightly browned and crispy and then set aside to cool completely. Then grind the walnuts using a food processor or blender.

2. Beat the eggs with the sugar using a hand mixer until the mixture becomes foamy and grows in volume at least two times.

3. Add the flour and beat the eggs mixture for 10 minutes more. Then mix in the baking powder.

4. Melt the cooking chocolate in a double boiler for 10 minutes and then stir in the other ingredients and mix well using a hand mixer.

5. Preheat the oven to 280°-300° Fahrenheit and then coat the parchment paper with the baking spray.

6. Spoon the mixture on the parchment paper and bake for around 40 minutes and then cut it into squares and you are free to serve. Remember that these mouth-watering and sweet walnut and vanilla brownies should be served warm.

Nutrients per serving:

Net Carbs: 11g; Total Fat: 19g; Protein: 9g; Calories: 182.8

19.   Gooseberry Orange Brownies

***Prep Time: 10 min | Cooking & Baking Time: 50
min | Servings: 4***

Ingredients:

- 1 cup of gooseberry jam

- 2 tablespoons orange zest, minced

- 1 tablespoon pure orange extract

- 5 tablespoons cocoa powder

- 5 tablespoons unsalted butter

- 3 eggs

- 1 cup of flour

- 1 cup of unsweetened cooking chocolate (70-95%)

- 2 teaspoons baking powder

- 3 tablespoons sugar

- 1 teaspoon vanilla

- baking spray

Instructions:

1. Combine the gooseberry jam with the half of the sugar and orange zest and mix the mixture using a spoon and then set aside for 30 minutes.

2. Beat the eggs with the sugar using a hand mixer until the mixture becomes foamy and grows in volume at least two times.

3. Add the flour and beat the eggs mixture for 10 minutes more. Then mix in the baking powder.

4. Melt the cooking chocolate in a double boiler for 10 minutes and add in the other ingredients and mix well using a hand mixer.

5. Preheat the oven to 280°-300° Fahrenheit and then coat the muffin cups or candy cups with the baking spray.

6. Pour the mixture into the muffin cups or candy cups and bake for around 40 minutes and then you are free to serve. Remember that these tasty gooseberry jam brownies should be served warm with the cup of hot chocolate.

Nutrients per serving:

Net Carbs: 11g; Total Fat: 24g; Protein: 9.9g; Calories: 182

20.   Orange Brownies

Prep Time: 10 min | Cooking & Baking Time: 50 min | Servings: 4

Ingredients:

- 1 cup of orange jam
- 2 tablespoons orange zest, minced
- 1 tablespoon pure orange extract
- 5 tablespoons cocoa powder
- 5 tablespoons unsalted butter
- 3 eggs
- 1 cup of flour
- 1 cup of unsweetened cooking chocolate (70-95%)
- 2 teaspoons baking powder
- 4 tablespoons sugar
- 1 teaspoon vanilla
- baking spray

Instructions:

1. Combine the orange jam with the half of the sugar and orange zest and mix the mixture using a spoon and then set aside for 30 minutes.

2. Beat the eggs with the sugar using a hand mixer until the mixture becomes foamy and grows in volume at least two times.

3. Add the flour and beat the eggs mixture for 10 minutes more. Then mix in the baking powder.

4. Melt the cooking chocolate in a double boiler for 10 minutes and add in the other ingredients and mix well using a hand mixer.

5. Preheat the oven to 280°-300° Fahrenheit and then coat the baking pan with the baking spray.

6. Pour the mixture into the baking pan and bake for around 40 minutes and then cut it into squares and you are free to serve. Remember that these tasty orange jam brownies should be served warm with the cup of hot chocolate.

Nutrients per serving:

Net Carbs: 12g; Total Fat: 25g; Protein: 9g; Calories: 183

21.   Almond Brownies

Prep Time: 10 min | Cooking & Baking Time: 50 min | Servings: 4

Ingredients:

- 1 cup of almonds

- 1 tablespoon pure almond extract

- 5 tablespoons cocoa powder

- 5 tablespoons unsalted butter

- 3 eggs

- 1 cup of almond flour

- 1 cup of unsweetened cooking chocolate (70-95%)

- 2 teaspoons baking powder

- 4 tablespoons sugar

- 1 teaspoon vanilla

- baking spray

Instructions:

1. Preheat the oven to 300°-320°Fahrenheit and roast the almonds in the oven for 10 minutes until lightly browned and crispy and then set aside to cool completely. Then grind the almonds using a food processor or blender.

2. Combine the pure almond extract with the half of the sugar and mix the mixture using a spoon and then set aside for 30 minutes.

3. Beat the eggs with the sugar using a hand mixer until the mixture becomes foamy and grows in volume at least two times.

4. Add the almond flour and beat the eggs mixture for 10 minutes more. Then mix in the baking powder.

5. Melt the cooking chocolate in a double boiler for 10 minutes and stir in the other ingredients and mix well using a hand mixer.

6. Preheat the oven to 280°-300° Fahrenheit and then coat the muffin cups or candy cups with the baking spray.

7. Pour the mixture into the muffin cups or candy cups and bake for around 30 minutes and then you are free to serve. Remember that these delicious almond brownies should be served warm with the cup of hot chocolate.

Nutrients per serving:

Net Carbs: 13g; Total Fat: 26g; Protein: 10g; Calories: 184

22. Pecan Raspberry Brownies

Prep Time: 10 min | Cooking & Baking Time: 50 min | Servings: 4

Ingredients:

- 1 cup of pecans
- 1 cup of fresh raspberries
- 1 tablespoon pure raspberry extract
- 5 tablespoons cocoa powder
- 5 tablespoons unsalted butter
- 3 eggs
- 1 cup of almond flour
- 1 cup of unsweetened cooking chocolate (70-95%)

- 2 teaspoons baking powder
- 4 tablespoons sugar
- 1 teaspoon vanilla
- baking spray

Instructions:

1. Preheat the oven to 300°-320°Fahrenheit and roast the pecans in the oven for 10 minutes until lightly browned and crispy and then set aside to cool completely. Then grind the pecans using a food processor or blender.

2. Combine the pure raspberry extract with the half of the sugar and mix the mixture using a spoon and then set aside for 30 minutes.

3. Beat the eggs with the sugar using a hand mixer until the mixture becomes foamy and grows in volume at least two times.

4. Add the almond flour and beat the eggs mixture for 10 minutes more. Then mix in the baking powder.

5. Melt the cooking chocolate in a double boiler for 10 minutes and stir in the other ingredients and mix well using a hand mixer.

6. Preheat the oven to 280°-300° Fahrenheit and then coat the muffin cups or candy cups with the baking spray.

7. Pour the mixture into the muffin cups or candy cups and bake for around 30 minutes and then you are free to serve. Remember that these delicious pecan raspberry brownies should be served warm with the cup of hot chocolate.

Nutrients per serving:

Net Carbs: 13.5g; Total Fat: 25g; Protein: 9g; Calories: 182

23.   Pecan Strawberry Brownies

Prep Time: 10 min | Cooking & Baking Time: 50 min | Servings: 4

Ingredients:

- 1 cup of pecans
- 1 cup of fresh and small strawberries
- 1 tablespoon pure strawberry extract
- 5 tablespoons cocoa powder
- 5 tablespoons unsalted butter
- 3 eggs
- 1 cup of flour
- 1 cup of unsweetened cooking chocolate (70-95%)
- 2 teaspoons baking powder
- 4 tablespoons sugar
- 1 teaspoon vanilla
- baking spray

Instructions:

1. Preheat the oven to 300°-320°Fahrenheit and roast the pecans in the oven for 10 minutes until lightly browned and crispy and then set aside to cool completely. Then grind the pecans using a food processor or blender.

2. Mash the strawberries using a potato masher. Combine the pure strawberry extract and mashed strawberries with the half of the sugar and mix the mixture using a spoon and then set aside for 30 minutes.

3. Beat the eggs with the sugar using a hand mixer until the mixture becomes foamy and grows in volume at least two times.

4. Add the flour and beat the eggs mixture for 10 minutes more. Then mix in the baking powder.

5. Melt the cooking chocolate in a double boiler for 10 minutes and stir in the other ingredients and mix well using a hand mixer.

6. Preheat the oven to 280°-300° Fahrenheit and then coat the baking pan with the baking spray.

7. Pour the mixture into the baking pan and bake for around 30 minutes and then cut it into squares and you are free to serve. Remember that these pecan strawberry brownies should be served cold with the cup of tea.

Nutrients per serving:

Net Carbs: 13.9g; Total Fat: 26.2g; Protein: 10g; Calories: 184

24. Pecan Peach Brownies

Prep Time: 10 min | Cooking & Baking Time: 50 min | Servings: 4

Ingredients:

- 5 peaches
- 1 tablespoon pure peach extract
- 5 tablespoons cocoa powder
- 5 tablespoons unsalted butter
- 3 eggs
- 1 cup of pecans
- 1 cup of flour

- 1 cup of unsweetened cooking chocolate (70-95%)

- 2 teaspoons baking powder

- 4 tablespoons sugar

- 1 teaspoon vanilla

- baking spray

Instructions:

1. Preheat the oven to 300°-320°Fahrenheit and roast the pecans in the oven for 10 minutes until lightly browned and crispy and then set aside to cool completely. Then grind the pecans using a food processor or blender.

2. Cube the peaches. Combine the pure peach extract and cubed peaches with the half of the sugar and mash the mixture using a potato masher and then set aside for 30 minutes.

3. Beat the eggs with the sugar using a hand mixer until the mixture becomes foamy and grows in volume at least two times.

4. Add the flour and beat the eggs mixture for 10 minutes more. Then mix in the baking powder.

5. Melt the cooking chocolate in a double boiler for 10 minutes and stir in the other ingredients and mix well using a hand mixer.

6. Preheat the oven to 280°-300° Fahrenheit and then coat the muffin cups or candy cups with the baking spray.

7. Pour the mixture into the muffin cups or candy cups and bake for around 30 minutes and then you are free to serve. Remember that these pecan peach brownies should be served cold with the cup of tea.

Nutrients per serving:

Net Carbs: 13g; Total Fat: 26g; Protein: 10g; Calories: 184

25. Wild Strawberry Brownies

Prep Time: 10 min | Cooking & Baking Time: 50 min | Servings: 4

Ingredients:

- 1 cup of wild strawberries

- 5 tablespoons wild strawberry (alpine strawberry) jam

- 2 teaspoons pure vanilla extract

- 5 tablespoons cocoa powder

- 5 tablespoons unsalted butter

- 3 eggs

- 1 cup of flour

- 1 cup of unsweetened cooking chocolate (70-95%)

- 2 teaspoons baking powder

- 4 tablespoons sugar

- baking spray

Instructions:

1. Mash the wild strawberries with the half of the sugar.

2. Combine the wild strawberry (alpine strawberry) jam with the mashed strawberries and mix the mixture using a spoon and then set aside for 30 minutes.

3. Beat the eggs with the sugar using a hand mixer until the mixture becomes foamy and grows in volume at least two times.

4. Add the flour and beat the eggs mixture for 10 minutes more. Then mix in the baking powder.

5. Melt the cooking chocolate in a double boiler for 10 minutes and add in the other ingredients and mix well using a hand mixer.

6. Preheat the oven to 280°-300° Fahrenheit and then coat the muffin cups or candy cups with the baking spray.

7. Pour the mixture into the muffin cups or candy cups and bake for around 40 minutes and then you are free to serve. Remember that these tasty wild strawberry brownies should be served warm with the cup of hot chocolate or cocoa.

Nutrients per serving:

Net Carbs: 12.5g; Total Fat: 25g; Protein: 10g; Calories: 179

26. Cherry Brownies

Prep Time: 10 min | Cooking & Baking Time: 50 min | Servings: 6

Ingredients:

- 1 cup of cherries, pitted
- half cup of cherry jam
- 2 tablespoons pure cherry extract
- 5 tablespoons cocoa powder
- 5 tablespoons unsalted butter
- 3 eggs
- 1 cup of flour

- 2 teaspoons baking powder

- 4 tablespoons sugar

- baking spray

Instructions:

1. Combine the cherry jam with the half of the sugar and mix the mixture using a spoon and then set aside for 30 minutes.

2. Beat the eggs with the sugar using a hand mixer until the mixture becomes foamy and grows in volume at least two times.

3. Add the flour and beat the eggs mixture for 10 minutes more. Then mix in the baking powder.

4. Combine all the ingredients and stir in the pitted cherries.

5. Preheat the oven to 280°-300° Fahrenheit and then coat the muffin cups or candy cups with the baking spray.

6. Pour the mixture into the muffin cups or candy cups and bake for around 40 minutes and then you are free to serve. Remember that these cherry brownies should be served warm with the cup of hot chocolate or cocoa.

Nutrients per serving:

Net Carbs: 12.5g; Total Fat: 25g; Protein: 10g; Calories: 179

27. Orange Cherry Brownies

Prep Time: 10 min | Cooking & Baking Time: 50 min | Servings: 6

Ingredients:

- 1 cup of cherries, pitted
- 2 tablespoons pure cherry extract
- 2 tablespoons pure orange extract
- 2 tablespoons orange zest, minced
- 5 tablespoons cocoa powder
- 5 tablespoons unsalted butter
- 3 eggs
- 1 cup of flour
- 2 teaspoons baking powder
- 4 tablespoons sugar
- baking spray

Instructions:

1. Combine the cherries with the half of the sugar and mash the berries using a potato masher and then set aside for 30 minutes.

2. Beat the eggs with the sugar using a hand mixer until the mixture becomes foamy and grows in volume at least two times.

3. Add the flour and beat the eggs mixture for 10 minutes more. Then mix in the baking powder.

4. Combine all the ingredients and stir in the pitted cherries.

5. Preheat the oven to 280°-300° Fahrenheit and then coat the baking pan with the baking spray.

6. Pour the mixture into the baking pan and bake for around 40 minutes and then cut it into squares and you are free to serve. Remember that these orange cherry brownies should be served warm with the cup of hot chocolate or cocoa.

Nutrients per serving:

Net Carbs: 12.9g; Total Fat: 26.2g; Protein: 11.3g; Calories: 178

28. Orange Coconut Brownies

Prep Time: 10 min. | Cooking Time: 35 min. | Servings: 6

Ingredients:

- 1 cup of walnuts
- 2 tablespoons orange zest, minced
- half cup of coconut oil
- 7 oz cocoa butter
- 7 tablespoons cocoa powder
- 1 tablespoon baking powder
- 1 cup of sugar
- 1 teaspoon vanilla

- 1 teaspoon coconut, shredded

- baking spray

Instructions:

1. Preheat the oven to 300°-320°Fahrenheit and roast the walnuts in the oven for 10 minutes until lightly browned and crispy. Then grind the walnuts using a food processor and set aside.

2. In a bowl, combine the cocoa powder, baking powder, and vanilla.

3. Melt the cocoa butter in a skillet for 5 minutes and then add in the sugar, coconut oil, and minced orange zest.

4. Combine the cocoa powder, baking powder and vanilla mixture with the melted cocoa butter mixture. Place the mix into a food processor and stir in the walnuts and shredded coconut. Mix all the ingredients until smooth consistency and homogenous mass.

5. Preheat the oven to 280°-300° Fahrenheit and then coat the muffin cups or candy cups with the baking spray.

6. Spoon the mixture into the muffin cups or candy cups and bake for 30 minutes.

7. Cool the orange coconut brownie muffins and then serve. Remember that this dessert should be served cold with the powdered sugar on top.

Nutrients per serving:

Net Carbs: 12.5g; Total Fat: 16.9g; Protein: 9g; Calories: 140

29. Lemon Coconut Brownies

Prep Time: 10 min. | *Cooking Time: 35 min.* | *Servings: 6*

Ingredients:

- 1 cup of walnuts
- 2 tablespoons lemon zest, minced
- half cup of coconut oil
- 7 oz cocoa butter
- 7 tablespoons cocoa powder
- 1 tablespoon baking powder
- 1 cup of sugar
- 1 teaspoon vanilla
- 1 teaspoon coconut, shredded
- baking spray

Instructions:

1. Preheat the oven to 300°-320°Fahrenheit and roast the walnuts in the oven for 10 minutes until lightly browned and crispy. Then grind the walnuts using a food processor and set aside.

2. In a bowl, combine the cocoa powder, baking powder, and vanilla.

3. Melt the cocoa butter in a skillet for 5 minutes and then add in the sugar, coconut oil, and minced lemon zest.

4. Combine the cocoa powder, baking powder and vanilla mixture with the melted cocoa butter mixture. Place the mix into a food processor and stir in the walnuts and shredded coconut. Mix all the ingredients until smooth consistency and homogenous mass.

5. Preheat the oven to 280°-300° Fahrenheit and then coat the muffin cups or candy cups with the baking spray.

6. Spoon the mixture into the muffin cups or candy cups and bake for 30 minutes.

7. Cool the lemon coconut brownie muffins and then serve. Remember that this dessert should be served cold with the powdered sugar on top.

Nutrients per serving:

Net Carbs: 12.5g; Total Fat: 16.9g; Protein: 9g; Calories: 140

30. Apricot Coconut Brownies

Prep Time: 10 min | Cooking & Baking Time: 50 min | Servings: 4

Ingredients:

- 1 cup of apricot jam

- 1 tablespoon pure apricot extract

- 5 tablespoons cocoa powder

- 5 tablespoons unsalted butter

- 7 oz cocoa butter

- 3 eggs

- 1 cup of flour

- 1 cup of unsweetened cooking chocolate (70-95%)

- 2 teaspoons baking powder

- 4 tablespoons sugar

- 1 teaspoon vanilla

- 2 teaspoons shredded coconut

- baking spray

Instructions:

1. Combine the apricot jam with the half of the sugar and pure apricot extract and mix the mixture using a spoon and then set aside for 30 minutes.

2. Beat the eggs with the sugar using a hand mixer until the mixture becomes foamy and grows in volume at least two times.

3. Add the flour and beat the eggs mixture for 10 minutes more. Then mix in the baking powder.

4. Combine all the ingredients except for the unsweetened cooking chocolate and mix well using a hand mixer.

5. Preheat the oven to 280°-300° Fahrenheit and then coat the baking pan with the baking spray.

6. Pour the mixture into the baking pan and bake for around 40 minutes.

7. Melt the cooking chocolate in a double boiler for 10 minutes and then cool. Pour the chocolate over the mixture and cut it into squares. Remember that these tasty apricot coconut brownies should be served warm with the cup of the hot chocolate.

Nutrients per serving:

Net Carbs: 13g; Total Fat: 26g; Protein: 10g; Calories: 184

31.   Peach Coconut Brownies

Prep Time: 10 min | Cooking & Baking Time: 50 min | Servings: 4

Ingredients:

- 1 cup of peach jam
- 1 tablespoon pure peach extract
- 5 tablespoons cocoa powder
- 5 tablespoons unsalted butter
- 7 oz cocoa butter
- 3 eggs
- 1 cup of flour
- 1 cup of unsweetened cooking chocolate (70-95%)
- 2 teaspoons baking powder
- 4 tablespoons sugar
- 1 teaspoon vanilla
- 2 teaspoons shredded coconut
- baking spray

Instructions:

1. Combine the peach jam with the half of the sugar and pure peach extract and mix the mixture using a spoon and then set aside for 30 minutes.

2. Beat the eggs with the sugar using a hand mixer until the mixture becomes foamy and grows in volume at least two times.

3. Add the flour and beat the eggs mixture for 10 minutes more. Then mix in the baking powder.

4. Combine all the ingredients except for the unsweetened cooking chocolate and mix well using a hand mixer.

5. Preheat the oven to 280°-300° Fahrenheit and then coat the muffin cups or candy cups with the baking spray.

6. Pour the mixture into the muffin cups or candy cups and bake for around 40 minutes.

7. Melt the cooking chocolate in a double boiler for 10 minutes and then cool. Pour the chocolate over the peach coconut brownies. Remember that these tasty peach coconut brownies should be served warm with the cup of the hot chocolate.

Nutrients per serving:

Net Carbs: 13.5g; Total Fat: 27g; Protein: 11g; Calories: 185

32.   Banana Coconut Brownies

Prep Time: 10 min | Cooking & Baking Time: 50 min | Servings: 4

Ingredients:

- 1 banana
- 1 cup of banana jam
- 2 tablespoons pure banana extract
- 5 tablespoons cocoa powder
- 5 tablespoons unsalted butter
- 7 oz cocoa butter
- 3 eggs
- 1 cup of flour

- 1 cup of unsweetened cooking chocolate (70-95%)

- 2 teaspoons baking powder

- 4 tablespoons sugar

- 1 teaspoon vanilla

- 2 teaspoons shredded coconut

- baking spray

Instructions:

1. Combine the banana jam with the half of the sugar and pure banana extract and mix the mixture using a spoon and then set aside for 30 minutes.

2. Beat the eggs with the sugar using a hand mixer until the mixture becomes foamy and grows in volume at least two times.

3. Add the flour and beat the eggs mixture for 10 minutes more. Then mix in the baking powder.

4. Combine all the ingredients except for the unsweetened cooking chocolate and mix well using a hand mixer.

5. Preheat the oven to 280°-300° Fahrenheit and then coat the baking pan with the baking spray.

6. Pour the mixture into the baking pan and bake for around 40 minutes.

7. Peel and cut the banana into rings and place on top of the mixture.

8. Melt the cooking chocolate in a double boiler for 10 minutes and then cool. Pour the chocolate over the banana coconut brownie mixture and cut it into squares. Remember that these banana coconut brownies should be served warm with the cup of the hot chocolate.

Nutrients per serving:

Net Carbs: 13.8g; Total Fat: 28g; Protein: 12g; Calories: 186

33. Pineapple Coconut Brownies

Prep Time: 10 min | Cooking & Baking Time: 50 min | Servings: 4

Ingredients:

- 1 cup of cubed pineapple
- 2 tablespoons pure pineapple extract
- 2 teaspoons pure coconut extract
- 5 tablespoons cocoa powder
- 5 tablespoons coconut butter
- 3 eggs
- 1 cup of flour
- 1 cup of unsweetened cooking chocolate (70-95%)
- 2 teaspoons baking powder
- 4 tablespoons sugar
- baking spray

Instructions:

1. Combine the cubed pineapple with the half of the sugar and then set aside for 30 minutes.

2. Beat the eggs with the sugar using a hand mixer until the mixture becomes foamy and grows in volume at least two times.

3. Add the flour and beat the eggs mixture for 10 minutes more. Then mix in the baking powder.

4. Melt the cooking chocolate in a double boiler for 10 minutes and then cool. Stir in the other ingredients and mix well using a hand mixer.

5. Preheat the oven to 280°-300° Fahrenheit and then coat the baking pan with the baking spray.

6. Pour the mixture into the baking pan and bake for around 40 minutes and then you are free to serve. Remember that these delicious pineapple coconut brownies should be served warm with the cup of hot chocolate or cocoa.

Nutrients per serving:

Net Carbs: 12g; Total Fat: 24g; Protein: 9.8g; Calories: 182

34. Raspberry Coconut Brownies

Prep Time: 10 min | Cooking & Baking Time: 55 min | Servings: 4

Ingredients:

- 1 cup of shredded coconut
- 1 cup of fresh raspberries
- 2 tablespoons pure raspberry extract
- 5 tablespoons cocoa powder
- 4 tablespoons unsalted butter
- 1 cup of unsweetened cooking chocolate (70-95%)
- 5 tablespoons coconut oil
- 2 teaspoons baking powder

- 5 tablespoons sugar

- 1 teaspoon vanilla

- baking spray

Instructions:

1. Preheat the oven to 300°-320°Fahrenheit and roast the shredded coconut in the oven for 5 minutes until lightly browned and then set aside to cool completely.

2. Combine the raspberries with the sugar and mash the berries using the potato masher. Then melt the cooking chocolate in a double boiler for 10 minutes and stir in the other ingredients and mix well using a hand mixer.

3. Preheat the oven to 280°-300° Fahrenheit and then coat the baking pan with the baking spray.

4. Pour the mixture into the baking pan and bake for around 40 minutes and then cut it into squares and you are free to serve. Remember that these delicious raspberry coconut brownies should be served warm with the cup of hot milk and honey.

Nutrients per serving:

Net Carbs: 13.5g; Total Fat: 25g; Protein: 10g; Calories: 194

35.   Strawberry Coconut Brownies

Prep Time: 10 min | Cooking & Baking Time: 55 min | Servings: 4

Ingredients:

- 1 cup of shredded coconut

- 2 cups of fresh strawberries

- 2 tablespoons pure strawberry extract

- 5 tablespoons cocoa powder

- 4 tablespoons unsalted butter

- 1 cup of unsweetened cooking chocolate (70-95%)

- 5 tablespoons coconut oil

- 2 teaspoons baking powder

- 5 tablespoons sugar

- 1 teaspoon vanilla

- baking spray

Instructions:

1. Preheat the oven to 300°-320°Fahrenheit and roast the shredded coconut in the oven for 5 minutes until lightly browned and then set aside to cool completely.

2. Combine the strawberries with the sugar and mash the berries using the potato masher. Then melt the cooking

chocolate in a double boiler for 10 minutes and stir in the other ingredients and mix well using a hand mixer.

3. Preheat the oven to 280°-300° Fahrenheit and then coat the muffin cups or candy cups with the baking spray.

4. Pour the mixture into the muffin cups or candy cups and bake for around 40 minutes and then you are free to serve. Remember that these delicious strawberry coconut brownies should be served warm with the cup of hot milk and honey.

Nutrients per serving:

Net Carbs: 13.8g; Total Fat: 26g; Protein: 11g; Calories: 192

36. Gooseberry Coconut Brownies

Prep Time: 10 min | Cooking & Baking Time: 55 min | Servings: 4

Ingredients:

- 1 cup of shredded coconut

- 2 cups of fresh gooseberries

- 4 tablespoons gooseberry jam

- 5 tablespoons cocoa powder

- 4 tablespoons unsalted butter

- 1 cup of unsweetened cooking chocolate (70-95%)

- 5 tablespoons coconut oil

- 2 teaspoons baking powder

- 5 tablespoons sugar

- 1 teaspoon vanilla

- baking spray

Instructions:

1. Preheat the oven to 300°-320°Fahrenheit and roast the shredded coconut in the oven for 5 minutes until lightly browned and then set aside to cool completely.

2. Combine the gooseberries with the sugar and mash the berries using the potato masher. Then melt the cooking chocolate in a double boiler for 10 minutes and stir in the other ingredients and mix well using a hand mixer.

3. Preheat the oven to 280°-300° Fahrenheit and then coat the muffin cups or candy cups with the baking spray.

4. Pour the mixture into the muffin cups or candy cups and bake for around 40 minutes and then you are free to serve. Remember that these delicious gooseberry coconut brownies should be served warm with the cup of tea.

Nutrients per serving:

Net Carbs: 13.9g; Total Fat: 26.5g; Protein: 11g; Calories: 189

37. Mango Walnut Brownies

Prep Time: 10 min | Cooking & Baking Time: 1 hour 10 min | Servings: 4

Ingredients:

- 1 cup of walnuts, ground
- 1 cup of mango, peeled and cubed
- 2 tablespoons pure mango extract
- 5 tablespoons cocoa powder
- 1 cup of unsweetened cooking chocolate (70-95%)
- 2 eggs
- 3 tablespoons unsalted butter
- 5 tablespoons sugar
- 1 teaspoon baking powder
- spray cream
- baking spray

Instructions:

1. Preheat the oven to 300°-320°Fahrenheit and roast the walnuts in the oven for 10 minutes until lightly browned and crispy and set aside to cool completely. Then grind the walnuts using a food processor.

2. Spoon the unsalted butter and sugar into a food processor and blend until homogenous mass. Then stir in the walnuts and mix well.

3. Mix in the pure mango extract, cocoa powder, eggs, and baking powder and blend all the ingredients using a food processor until they have a smooth and creamy consistency. Add in the mango cubes and mix until homogenous mass.

4. Melt the cooking chocolate in a double boiler for 10 minutes and then combine and mix all the ingredients well using a hand mixer.

5. Preheat the oven to 280°-300° Fahrenheit and then coat the silicone molds or muffin cups with the baking spray.

6. Spoon the sweet mango walnut brownies mixture into the silicone molds or muffin cups and bake for 50 minutes at 300°- 320°Fahrenheit.

7. Then cool the mango walnut brownies and serve with the spray cream on top. Remember that these tasty mango walnuts brownies should be served cool.

Nutrients per serving:

Net Carbs: 11.5g; Total Fat: 27g; Protein: 13g; Calories: 218

38. Pear Walnut Brownies

Prep Time: 10 min | Cooking & Baking Time: 1 hour 10 min | Servings: 4

Ingredients:

- 1 cup of walnuts, ground
- 2 cups of pears, peeled and cubed
- 1 teaspoon pure vanilla extract
- 5 tablespoons cocoa powder
- 1 cup of unsweetened cooking chocolate (70-95%)
- 2 eggs
- 3 tablespoons coconut butter
- 5 tablespoons sugar

- 1 teaspoon baking powder

- spray cream

- baking spray

Instructions:

1. Preheat the oven to 300°-320°Fahrenheit and roast the walnuts in the oven for 10 minutes until lightly browned and crispy and set aside to cool completely. Then grind the walnuts using a food processor.

2. Spoon the coconut butter and sugar into a food processor and blend until homogenous mass. Then stir in the walnuts and mix well.

3. Mix in the pure vanilla extract, cocoa powder, eggs, and baking powder and blend all the ingredients using a food processor until they have a smooth and creamy consistency. Add in the pears cubes and mix until homogenous mass.

4. Melt the cooking chocolate in a double boiler for 10 minutes and then stir in the other ingredients and mix well using a hand mixer.

5. Preheat the oven to 280°-300° Fahrenheit and then coat the silicone molds or muffin cups with the baking spray.

6. Spoon the sweet pear walnut brownies mixture into the silicone molds or muffin cups and bake for 50 minutes at 300°- 320°Fahrenheit.

7. Then cool the pear walnut brownies and serve with the spray cream on top. Remember that these tasty pear walnut brownies should be served cool.

Nutrients per serving:

Net Carbs: 10.5g; Total Fat: 28g; Protein: 16g; Calories: 259

39. Pear Peanut Brownies

Prep Time: 10 min | Cooking & Baking Time: 1 hour 10 min | Servings: 4

Ingredients:

- 1 cup of peanuts, ground
- 2 cups of pears, peeled and cubed
- 1 teaspoon pure vanilla extract
- 5 tablespoons cocoa powder
- 1 cup of unsweetened cooking chocolate (70-95%)
- 2 eggs
- 3 tablespoons coconut butter
- 5 tablespoons sugar
- 1 teaspoon baking powder
- spray cream
- baking spray

Instructions:

1. Preheat the oven to 300°-320°Fahrenheit and roast the peanuts in the oven for 10 minutes until lightly browned and crispy and set aside to cool completely. Then grind the peanuts using a food processor.

2. Spoon the coconut butter and sugar into a food processor and blend until homogenous mass. Then stir in the peanuts and mix well.

3. Mix in the pure vanilla extract, cocoa powder, eggs, and baking powder and blend all the ingredients using a food processor until they have a smooth and creamy consistency. Add in the pears cubes and mix until homogenous mass.

4. Melt the cooking chocolate in a double boiler for 10 minutes and then stir in the other ingredients and mix well using a hand mixer or food processor.

5. Preheat the oven to 280°-300° Fahrenheit and then coat the silicone molds or muffin cups with the baking spray.

6. Spoon the sweet pear peanut brownies mixture into the silicone molds or muffin cups and bake for 50 minutes at 300°- 320°Fahrenheit.

7. Then cool the pear peanut brownies and serve with the spray cream on top. Remember that these pear walnut brownies should be served cold with the cup of coffee.

Nutrients per serving:

Net Carbs: 10g; Total Fat: 27g; Protein: 16g; Calories: 258

40.   Peanut Honey Brownies

Prep Time: 10 min | Cooking & Baking Time: 50 min | Servings: 4

Ingredients:

- 1 cup of peanuts, ground
- 1 cup of honey
- 5 tablespoons cocoa powder
- 4 tablespoons unsalted butter
- 1 cup of unsweetened cooking chocolate (70-95%)
- 5 tablespoons coconut oil
- 2 teaspoons baking powder
- 5 tablespoons sugar

- 1 teaspoon cinnamon

- baking spray

Instructions:

1. Preheat the oven to 300°-320°Fahrenheit and roast the peanuts in the oven for 10 minutes until lightly browned and crispy and then set aside to cool completely. Then grind the peanuts using a food processor.

2. Melt the cooking chocolate in a double boiler for 10 minutes and then stir in the other ingredients and mix well using a hand mixer.

3. Preheat the oven to 280°-300° Fahrenheit and then coat the baking pan with the baking spray.

4. Pour the mixture into the baking pan and bake for around 40 minutes and then cut it into squares and you are free to serve. Remember that these delicious peanut honey brownies should be served cold with the glass of milk.

Nutrients per serving:

Net Carbs: 12.8g; Total Fat: 21g; Protein: 10g; Calories: 189

Conclusion

Thank you and I hope you have enjoyed this brownies cookbook.

Our collection of brownie recipes will be a great helper in your cooking routine. Bake tasty and healthy brownies for your friends or family!

If you've enjoyed this cookbook, I'd greatly appreciate if you could leave an honest review on Amazon.

Made in the USA
San Bernardino, CA
19 December 2019

61839364R00053